Enrichment

MATH

Dear Student,

Here is your Enrichment Math book. This book is filled with exciting math things to do at home. You will play games, work puzzles, have trivia quizzes and contests. Ask your family and friends to work with you on these activities.

While you are having fun, you will be learning math. We hope Enrichment Math will be one of your favorite things to do this year.

Good luck from your friends at Enrichment Math.

Peggy Kaye

Carole Greenes

Linda Schulman

Table of Contents

Target Sum

The number at the top of each sign is the target number. Draw a ring around three pairs of numbers whose sum is the target number.

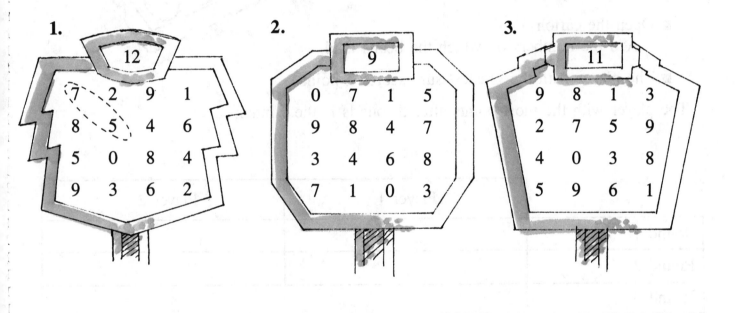

1. 12

7	2	9	1
8	5	4	6
5	0	8	4
9	3	6	2

2. 9

0	7	1	5
9	8	4	7
3	4	6	8
7	1	0	3

3. 11

9	8	1	3
2	7	5	9
4	0	3	8
5	9	6	1

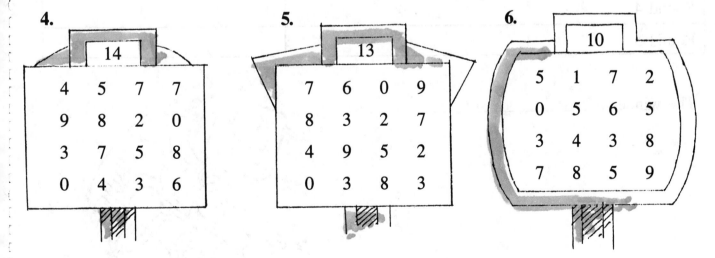

4. 14

4	5	7	7
9	8	2	0
3	7	5	8
0	4	3	6

5. 13

7	6	0	9
8	3	2	7
4	9	5	2
0	3	8	3

6. 10

5	1	7	2
0	5	6	5
3	4	3	8
7	8	5	9

Shake-A-Sum

Find an egg carton.

Write the numbers in the sections.

Ask someone to play this game with you.

Play 5 rounds.

In each round:

- Put 2 beans in the carton.
  Close the carton and shake it.

- Open the carton.
  Add the numbers on which the beans land.

- The player with the greatest sum scores a point.

The player with the most points after 5 rounds is the winner.

	Player 1	Player 2
Round 1		
Round 2		
Round 3		
Round 4		
Round 5		

The winner is _____

Match It Right

Use these numbers.
Put the correct number in the boxes below.
Cross off the number after you use it.

18   10
11   12
4   9   13
7
3   16
8
6   0   5

1.
$$\begin{array}{r} 17 \\ -9 \\ \hline \square \end{array}$$

2.
$$\begin{array}{r} 15 \\ -\square \\ \hline 9 \end{array}$$

3.
$$\begin{array}{r} 11 \\ -\square \\ \hline 7 \end{array}$$

4.
$$\begin{array}{r} \square \\ -9 \\ \hline 9 \end{array}$$

5.
$$\begin{array}{r} \square \\ -7 \\ \hline 6 \end{array}$$

6.
$$\begin{array}{r} 14 \\ -\square \\ \hline 5 \end{array}$$

7.
$$\begin{array}{r} \square \\ -8 \\ \hline 8 \end{array}$$

8.
$$\begin{array}{r} 2 \\ -\square \\ \hline 2 \end{array}$$

9.
$$\begin{array}{r} \square \\ -2 \\ \hline 9 \end{array}$$

10.
$$\begin{array}{r} 16 \\ -\square \\ \hline 9 \end{array}$$

11.
$$\begin{array}{r} \square \\ -5 \\ \hline 7 \end{array}$$

12.
$$\begin{array}{r} \square \\ -\square \\ \hline 3 \end{array}$$

Take 1-2-3

Here is a game for you and a friend.

- Make a pile of 15 chips or coins.

- Decide who plays first.

- Take turns.

- On your turn, take away, 1, 2, or 3 chips.

- The winner is the person who takes the last chip.

Play five games.

Keep track of the winners.

Game	Winner
1	_____
2	_____
3	_____
4	_____
5	_____

Who won more games?_____

Here are some questions for the winner.

1. Did you play first when you won?_____

2. What plan did you use to win?_____

_____

Subtracting with Basic Facts

Nines-By-Fingers

You can use your fingers to find the products when multiplying by nine.

Hold out both hands. Think of your fingers numbered 1 through 10.

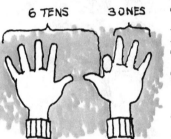

To find 7 × 9:
Put down finger number 7.
The number of fingers to the left is the number of tens.
The number of fingers to the right is the number of ones.

7 × 9 = 63

Use your fingers to find these products.

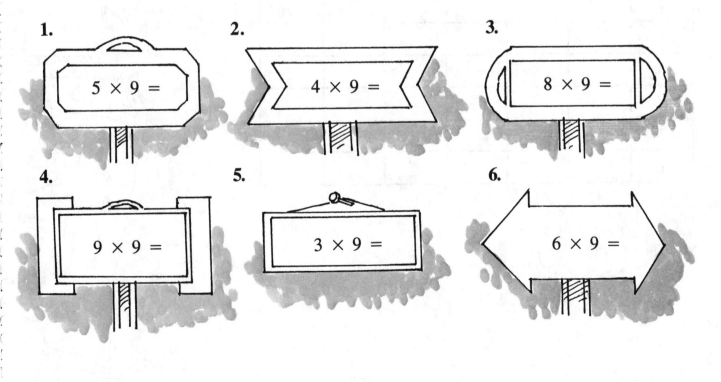

1.

5 × 9 =

2.

4 × 9 =

3.

8 × 9 =

4.

9 × 9 =

5.

3 × 9 =

6.

6 × 9 =

Roll-A-Product

Ask someone to play this game with you.

You need 2 number cubes and 2 crayons.

Take turns.

On each turn:

■ Roll 2 number cubes.

■ Multiply the two numbers you roll.

■ Write the product on the playing board if the space is empty.

The first player to write four products in the same row, column, or diagonal is the winner.

Example
I roll ⚁ ⚅.
I can write 12 in
the space for 2 × 6
or in the space
for 6 × 2.

Playing Board

×	1	2	3	4	5	6
1						
2						
3						
4						
5						
6						

2 × 6 =
12

6 × 2 =
12

Division Squares

Write the missing numbers.

Make true number sentences across and down.

1.

24	÷	6	=	
÷		÷		÷
8	÷	2	=	
=		=		=
	÷		=	

2.

36	÷	6	=	
÷		÷		÷
9	÷	3	=	
=		=		=
	÷		=	

3.

48	÷	6	=	
÷		÷		÷
8	÷	2	=	
=		=		=
	÷		=	

4.

40	÷	4	=	
÷		÷		÷
8	÷	4	=	
=		=		=
	÷		=	

How Many Please?

Take a look around your kitchen.

Have an adult help you.

1. What can you find that comes 2 in a package?

_____   _____

2. How many packages would you have to buy if you wanted 8 in all?_____

3. What can you find that comes 4 in a package?

_____   _____

4. How many packages would you have to buy if you wanted 20 in all?_____

5. What can you find that comes 6 in a package?

_____   _____

6. How many packages would you have to buy if you wanted 30 in all?_____

Dividing with Basic Facts

Number Sentence

Use the numbers on the sign.

Use addition, subtraction, multiplication, or division.

Write two number sentences that are true.

Example

$30 \div 5 = 6$

$10 - 6 = 4$

10	5
30	6

1.

_____ = 28

_____ = 54

6	4
9	7

2.

_____ = 16

_____ = 3

18	7
9	6

3.

_____ = 7

_____ = 4

9	12
13	5

4.

_____ = 3

_____ = 11

24	8
7	4

5.

_____ = 0

_____ = 6

8	36
6	0

Using Mixed Operations with Basic Facts

11

Get Four

Ask someone to play this game with you.

You need 2 number cubes and a pencil.

Take turns.

On each turn:

- Roll 2 number cubes.

- Add, subtract, or multiply the two numbers you roll.

- Write your initials in a square on the gameboard that shows the sum, difference, or product.

A square may have more than one player's initials.

The first player to initial four squares in the same row, column, or diagonal is the winner.

GAMEBOARD

15	5	20	10	3
36	9	0	25	2
7	24	4	12	11
1	16	8	7	30
0	10	18	6	9

Using Mixed Operations with Basic Facts

Cross Numbers

Use the operations +, −, ×, ÷.

Put an operation sign in each empty box.

Make true number sentences across and down.

1.

5		7	=	12
3		2	=	6
=		=		=
15		9	=	6

2.

18		6	=	3
2		4	=	8
=		=		=
9		2	=	11

3.

7		2	=	14
6		3	=	2
=		=		=
13		6	=	7

4.

24		3	=	8
6		2	=	3
=		=		=
4		1	=	5

Numbers Up

2, 3, or 4 people can play this game.

- Use cards.
  Make 10 number cards like these.

- Take turns.

- Mix up the cards and place them face down.

- Pick two cards.

- Use the numbers and +, −, × or ÷.
  Write a number sentence.

  If the answer is greater than 30, score 2 points.

  If the answer is less than 10, score 2 points.

  If the answer is between 10 and 30, score 1 point.

- Mix up the cards again before the next player's turn.

SCORE 2 POINTS

After six turns, the player with the highest score is the winner.

Players:				
Turn 1				
Turn 2				
Turn 3				
Turn 4				
Turn 5				
Turn 6				
Total Score				

Using Mixed Operations with Basic Facts

Big Numbers

Find the BIG NUMBER. Use the clues to help you.

1. Use 2, 3, 7, 8.
Clues:
■ The 2 is in the ones place.
■ The 7 is in the hundreds place.
■ The 8 is in the tens place.
■ The 3 is in the thousands place.
BIG NUMBER ☐☐☐☐

2. Use 5, 0, 9, 4.
Clues:
■ The greatest number is in the tens place.
■ The smallest number is in the ones place.
■ The number in the thousands place is less than the number in the hundreds place.
BIG NUMBER ☐☐☐☐

3. Use 9, 5, 2, 8.
Clues:
■ The greatest number is in the thousands place.
■ The smallest number is in the ones place.
■ The number in the hundreds place is greater than the number in the tens place.
BIG NUMBER ☐☐☐☐

4. Use 1, 6, 2, 7.
Clues:
■ The number in the hundreds place is 4 more than the number in the tens place.
■ The greatest number is in the ones place.
BIG NUMBER ☐☐☐☐

5. Use 3, 5, 6, 4.
Clues:
■ The 5 is in the hundreds place.
■ The sum of the numbers in the hundreds place and the ones place is nine.
■ The number in the tens place is less than the number in the hundreds place.
BIG NUMBER ☐☐☐☐

6. Use 7, 1, 0, 9.
Clues:
■ The number in the ones place is 6 more than the number in the hundreds place.
■ The number in the thousands place is 9 more than the number in the tens place.
BIG NUMBER ☐☐☐☐

Place It Right

2, 3, or 4 people can play this game.

■ Make 9 number cards like these.

■ Mix up the cards and place them face down.

■ Each player draws these boxes on a sheet of paper.

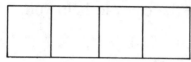

■ Turn over one card.
Each player writes the number in one of the boxes.

■ Turn over another card.
Each player writes the number in one of the boxes.

■ Do this two more times.

■ Compare the numbers.

The player with the greatest number is the winner.

Challenge Question:

Use the same four number cards. How many different numbers can you make? _____

Show the numbers here.

Using Place Value to Thousands

Tiny Toys

Round each price to the nearest dollar.

Tell what each person bought.

1. 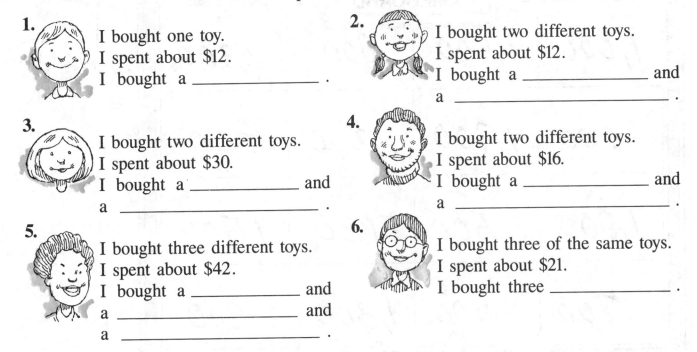 I bought one toy.
I spent about $12.
I bought a _____ .

2. I bought two different toys.
I spent about $12.
I bought a _____ and
a _____ .

3. I bought two different toys.
I spent about $30.
I bought a _____ and
a _____ .

4. I bought two different toys.
I spent about $16.
I bought a _____ and
a _____ .

5. I bought three different toys.
I spent about $42.
I bought a _____ and
a _____ and
a _____ .

6. I bought three of the same toys.
I spent about $21.
I bought three _____ .

Rounding Bingo

Here's a game for you and your friend.

Rules

- Take turns.
- Pick two numbers from the sign.
- Round each number to the nearest hundred.
- Add the rounded numbers.
- Mark the answer on the game board. Use your **X** or **O**.

1,401	358
275	109
899	521

X_____ **O**_____

The first player with four **X**s or **O**s in a row, column, or diagonal is the winner.

GAMEBOARD

1,000	1,900	800	2,300
1,400	1,700	1,200	400
1,800	500	FREE	1,500
700	600	1,300	900

Tic-Tac-Sum

172   10

258   424

20

Pick any two of these numbers.

Add the two numbers. Use the work space.

Put an **X** on the sum.

When you get three **X**s in a row, stop!

430	682	182
444	596	268
278	434	~~192~~

Work Space

172
+ 20
———
192

100   510

390   50

840

Try again. Use these numbers.

Can you get three **X**s in a row with fewer tries?

440	940	1,230
610	900	560
890	1,350	490

Work Space

Adding 2- to 4-Digit Numbers

The Largest-Smallest Trivia Quiz

Here's a quiz for you and your family.
First try to answer the question.
Then add.
Ring the sum. The sum gives the answer to the question.

1. What is the largest fish
in the world?

102	cod	43
112	whale shark	+ 69
113	tuna	
1,012	sea bass	

2. What is the smallest
fish in the world?

1,843	guppy	1,564
1,743	goldfish	+ 289
1,753	angelfish	
1,853	goby	

3. What is the largest bird
in the world?

133	turkey	128
113	parrot	+ 15
161	penguin	
143	ostrich	

4. What is the smallest
bird in the world?

1,190	parakeet	505
1,290	robin	+ 695
1,200	Helena's hummingbird	
1,195	bluejay	

5. What is the largest dog
in the world?

616	St. Bernard	236
516	golden retriever	+ 380
556	collie	
510	Great Dane	

6. What is the smallest dog
in the world?

7,000	Yorkshire terrier	3,192
6,990	toy poodle	+ 3,808
6,900	chihuahua	
6,910	bull dog	

Adding 2- to 4-Digit Numbers

Cross-Number Puzzle

LESSON
10

Subtract.
Write the differences in the cross-number puzzle.

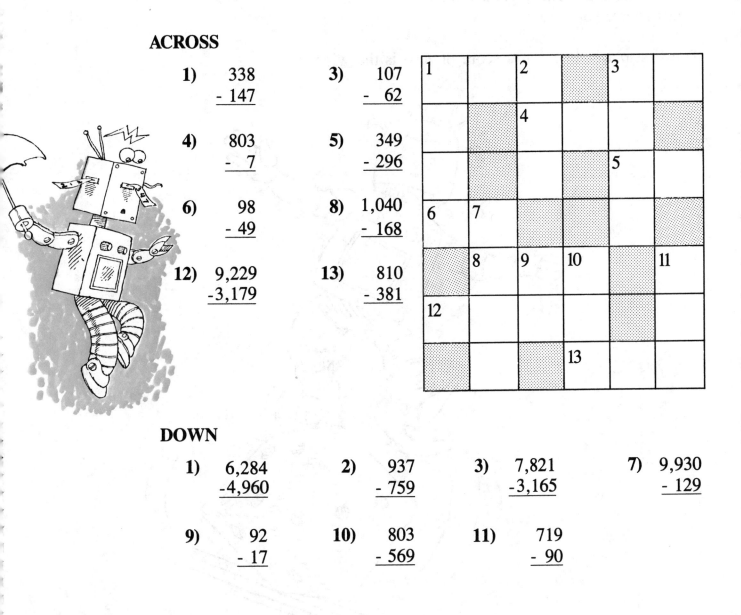

ACROSS

1) 338
   - 147

3) 107
   - 62

4) 803
   - 7

5) 349
   - 296

6) 98
   - 49

8) 1,040
   - 168

12) 9,229
    -3,179

13) 810
    - 381

DOWN

1) 6,284
   -4,960

2) 937
   - 759

3) 7,821
   -3,165

7) 9,930
   - 129

9) 92
   - 17

10) 803
    - 569

11) 719
    - 90

Subtracting 2- to 4-Digit Numbers

199

This is a game for you and a friend.
Each player starts with a score of 199.

Take turns.
On each turn:

■ Roll 1 or 2 number cubes.

■ Use the number cubes to make a number.

■ Subtract the number from your score.

■ If you make a number greater than
your score, you lose.

The first player to reach a score of zero is the winner.

Estimating Products

Pick a number from the cloud to make the sentence true.

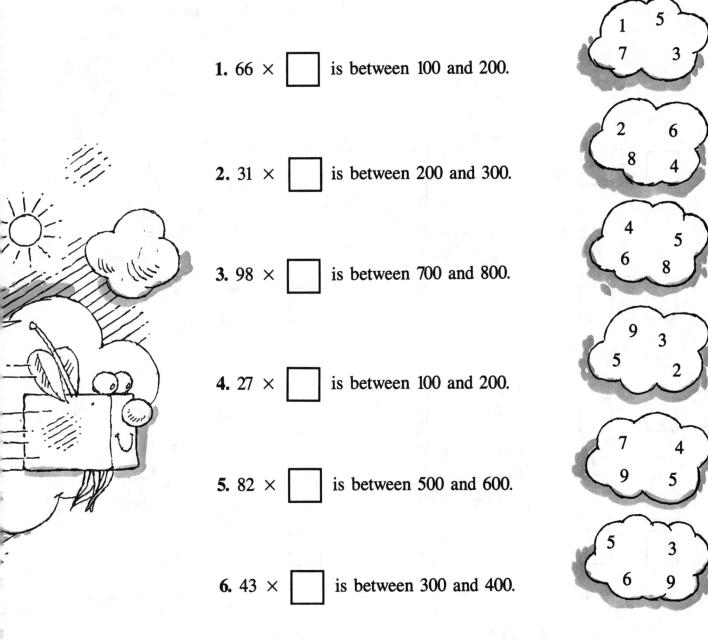

1. 66 × ☐ is between 100 and 200.

2. 31 × ☐ is between 200 and 300.

3. 98 × ☐ is between 700 and 800.

4. 27 × ☐ is between 100 and 200.

5. 82 × ☐ is between 500 and 600.

6. 43 × ☐ is between 300 and 400.

Multiplying 2-Digit Numbers by 1-Digit Numbers

Multiplication Puzzle

Find a friend who likes to solve puzzles.

Work together to make multiplication examples that are true.

Use each of the numbers on the sign.

It may help to write the numbers on pieces of paper. Then you can move the numbers around until you place them correctly.

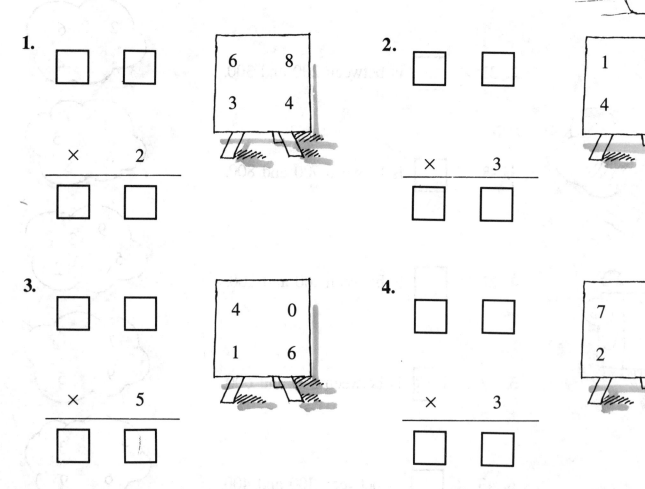

1.

☐ ☐

```
6    8
3    4
```

× 2

☐ ☐

2.

☐ ☐

```
1    5
4    5
```

× 3

☐ ☐

3.

☐ ☐

```
4    0
1    6
```

× 5

☐ ☐

4.

☐ ☐

```
7    8
2    6
```

× 3

☐ ☐

Multiplying 2-Digit Numbers by 1-Digit Numbers

Teeth Totals

Divide.

The answer gives you a fact about teeth.

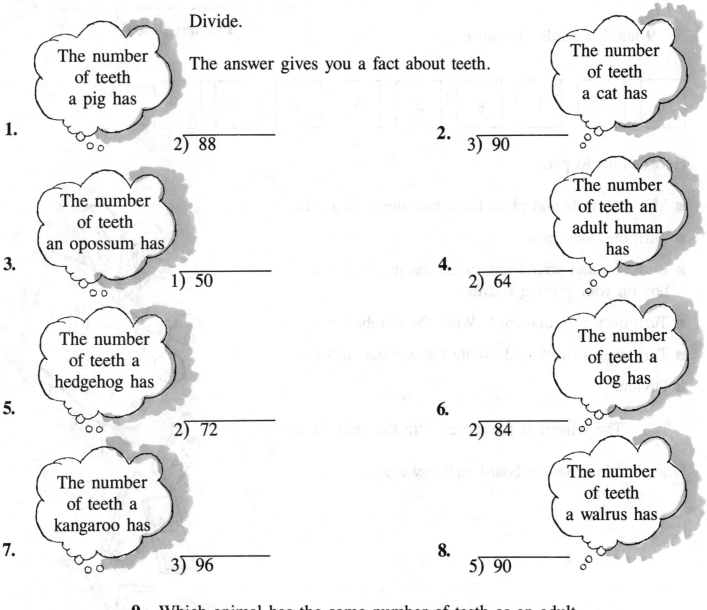

The number
of teeth
a pig has

1.

2) 88

The number
of teeth
a cat has

2.

3) 90

The number
of teeth
an opossum has

3.

1) 50

The number
of teeth an
adult human
has

4.

2) 64

The number
of teeth a
hedgehog has

5.

2) 72

The number
of teeth a
dog has

6.

2) 84

The number
of teeth a
kangaroo has

7.

3) 96

The number
of teeth
a walrus has

8.

5) 90

9. Which animal has the same number of teeth as an adult human?_____

10. Which animals have more teeth than an adult human? _____

_____

Divvy Up

Play Divvy Up with a friend.

You will need:

A playing board for each player.
You can draw the board on a sheet of paper.

9 number cards like these.

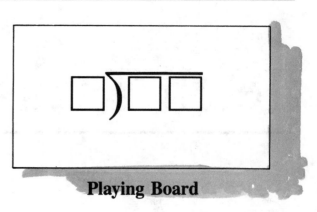

Playing Board

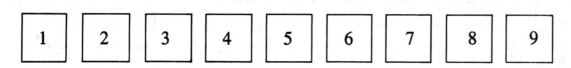

Here is how to play:

■ Mix the cards and place them face down in a pile.

■ Turn over one card.

■ Both you and your friend write the number in a box on your playing boards.

■ Turn over a second card. Write the number in a box.

■ Turn over a third card. Write the number in a box.

■ Divide.

The winner is the player with the greatest answer.

Draw another playing board and play again.

Dividing 2-Digit Numbers by 1-Digit Numbers

Arrow Path

Move around on the number board.

25↑ Means start at 25.
Move up one space.
You stop at 35.

43→ Means start at 43.
Move right one space.
You stop at 44.

6↑↑ Means start at 6.
Move up two spaces.
You stop at 26.

91	92	93	94	95	96	97	98	99	100
81	82	83	84	85	86	87	88	89	90
71	72	73	74	75	76	77	78	79	80
61	62	63	64	65	66	67	68	69	70
51	52	53	54	55	56	57	58	59	60
41	42	43	44	45	46	47	48	49	50
31	32	33	34	35	36	37	38	39	40
21	22	23	24	25	26	27	28	29	30
11	12	13	14	15	16	17	18	19	20
1	2	3	4	5	6	7	8	9	10

Write the missing numbers.

START	ARROWS	STOP
2	↑	
14	↑	
38	↑	
15	→	
31	→	
42	←	
57	←	
25	↓	
39	↓ →	
6	↑ ↑	
21	↓ → →	
80	↓ ↓ ↓ ←	
38	↑ ↑ ↑ →	

Write the missing arrows.

START	ARROWS	STOP
3		13
35		55
64		44
32		35
76		73
7		26
52		14
19		85
22		34
98		56
62		95
16		66
37		80

Magic Nines

Be a magician.

Cover your eyes.
Give these rules to an adult to follow.

■ Write down a three-digit number.

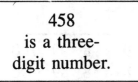

458
is a three-
digit number.

■ Use the same three digits to
write a different number.

I can write
845.

■ Subtract the smaller number from
the greater number.

■ Add the digits in the difference.
Keep adding digits until you get just one.

$$845$$
$$- 458$$
$$387$$

$$3 + 8 + 7 = 18$$
$$1 + 8 = 9$$

Now you say, ''Abrakadabrah, mollickymine.
        Your final answer is 9.''

Try it again!

Birthday Logic

October

Sunday	Monday	Tuesday	Wednesday	Thursday	Friday	Saturday
		1	2	3	4	5
6	7	8	9	10	11	12
13	14	15	16	17	18	19
20	21	22	23	24	25	26
27	28	29	30	31		

Use the calendar to help you find each person's birth date.

1. My birthday is on a Tuesday.
It is after October 2.
It is before October 14.
My birthday is October_____.

Karen

2. My birthday is on a Wednesday.
When you count by 5s you say
the number of my birth date.
My birthday is October_____.

Bob

3. My birthday is on a Tuesday.
My birthday is two weeks after
Karen's birthday.

My birthday is October_____.

4. My birthday is on a Sunday.
It is before Ted's birthday.
When you count by 3s you say
my birth date.
My birthday is October_____.

Ted

Carol

5. My birthday is on a weekend.
It is after Ted's birthday.
It is not a Sunday.
My birthday is October_____.

Sheila

6. My birthday is on a Monday.
The date is the number of days
in 3 weeks.
My birthday is October_____.

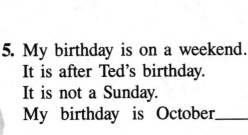

Dan

Seconds Count

Are you a good guesser?
To check it out, you'll need a friend to time you.
Your friend will need a watch or a timer that measures seconds.

Write down your guesses first.
Then do the tasks as your friend counts.
Fill in the count.

30-SECOND TASKS

How many times can you:	Guess	Count
clap your hands?		
tap your foot?		
jump up and down?		
write your telephone number?		

Draw a ring around your best guess.

60-SECOND TASKS

How many:	Guess	Count
animals can you name?		
foods can you name?		
states can you name?		
U.S. Presidents can you name?		

Draw a ring around your best guess.

Measure Up

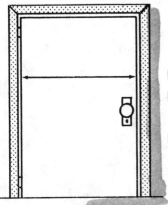

A doorway is about 1 meter wide.

■ Make a list of five objects.
■ Cut a piece of string one meter long. Use the string to check each object.
■ Put an **X** in the box that tells about the length of each object.

Object	Length		
	About one meter	More than one meter	Less then one meter
1.			
2.			
3.			
4.			
5.			

Which object was closest to one meter long?_____

Now use the string to see how you measure up.

You	Length		
	About one meter	More than one meter	Less than one meter
6. Height			
7. Leg			
8. Arm span			
9. Walking step			

Fish Quiz

This is a quiz for you and your family.

1 meter = 100 centimeters

The lengths of the saltwater fish are on the sign.
Use each number once. Read the clues to find the lengths of the
fish in centimeters.

91	300
400	
61	340
160	
270	46

1. The sailfish is 3 meters long.
   The sailfish is _____ centimeters long.

2. The Atlantic cod is 9 centimeters less than
   one meter long. The Atlantic cod is
   _____ centimeters long.

3. The great barracuda is 60 centimeters more
   than one meter long. The great barracuda
   is _____ centimeters long.

4. The bluefin tuna is
   2 meters 70 centimeters long.
   The bluefin tuna is _____ centimeters long.

5. The ocean sunfish is 3 meters 40 centimeters
   long. The ocean sunfish is _____ centimeters
   long.

6. The swordfish is 1 meter longer than
   the sailfish. The swordfish is
   _____ centimeters long.

7. The bluefish is 11 centimeters more than
   half a meter long. The bluefish is
   _____ centimeters long.

8. The black sea bass is 4 centimeters less
   than half a meter long. The black sea
   bass is _____ centimeters long.

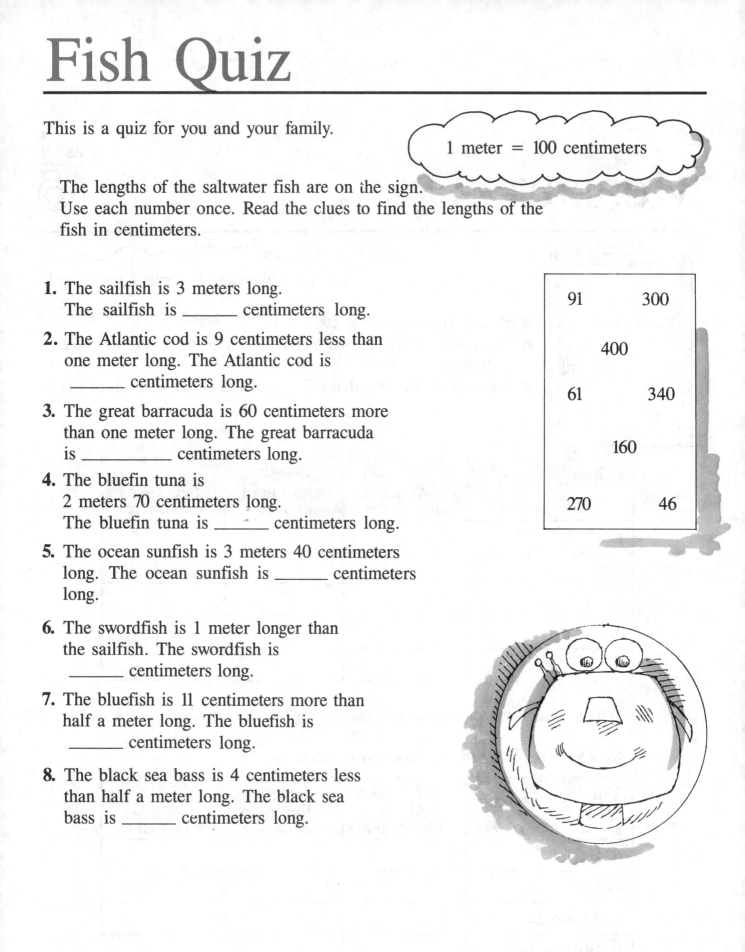

Measurement Sense

Use each unit in the sign once. Make sure the measurements make sense.

inches	pounds
ounces	hours
quart	days
miles	feet
years	minutes

1. Marcie is 9 _____ old.

2. She is 50 _____ tall and weighs 56 _____ .

3. Her brother, Paul, is 4 _____ tall.

4. Paul is 365 _____ younger than Marcie.

5. Marcie drinks 8 _____ of orange juice each morning and 1 _____ of milk every day.

6. Marcie and Paul ride their bicycles 2 _____ to school.

7. It takes them about 15 _____ to ride to school.

8. They go to school for 6 _____ each day.

Measures In The Kitchen

Take a look in your kitchen or in a store.

Ask an adult to help you.

1. What can you find that is measured in pounds? _____
How many pounds?

_____   _____   _____

2. What can you find that is measured in ounces? _____

How many ounces?

_____   _____   _____

3. What can you find that is measured in quarts? _____
How many quarts?

_____   _____   _____

4. What can you find that is measured in gallons? _____
How many gallons?

_____   _____   _____

Using Customary Units

Graph Pictures

Graph each point.

Connect the points in order.

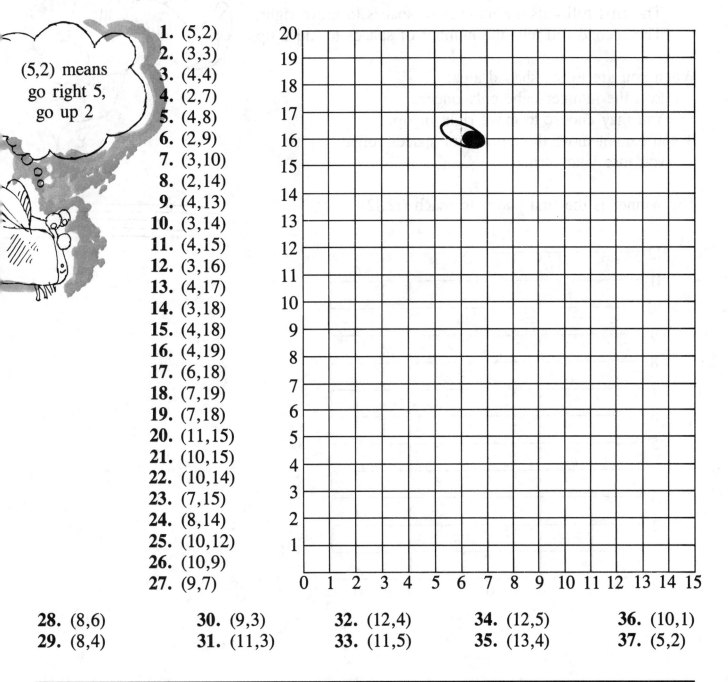

(5,2) means
go right 5,
go up 2

1. (5,2)
2. (3,3)
3. (4,4)
4. (2,7)
5. (4,8)
6. (2,9)
7. (3,10)
8. (2,14)
9. (4,13)
10. (3,14)
11. (4,15)
12. (3,16)
13. (4,17)
14. (3,18)
15. (4,18)
16. (4,19)
17. (6,18)
18. (7,19)
19. (7,18)
20. (11,15)
21. (10,15)
22. (10,14)
23. (7,15)
24. (8,14)
25. (10,12)
26. (10,9)
27. (9,7)

28. (8,6)
29. (8,4)
30. (9,3)
31. (11,3)
32. (12,4)
33. (11,5)
34. (12,5)
35. (13,4)
36. (10,1)
37. (5,2)

The (12,12) Race

Ask someone to play this game with you.
You need a number cube and 2 markers.

■ Each player begins at (0, 0).

■ Take turns.

■ On each turn:
   Roll the number cube two times.
   The first roll tells the number of spaces to move right.
   The second roll tells the number of spaces to move up.

When you are in the shaded area:
   Roll the number cube only once.
   You may choose to move right or up.
If you cannot move the number of spaces rolled,
   you lose your turn.

The winner is the first player to reach (12,12).

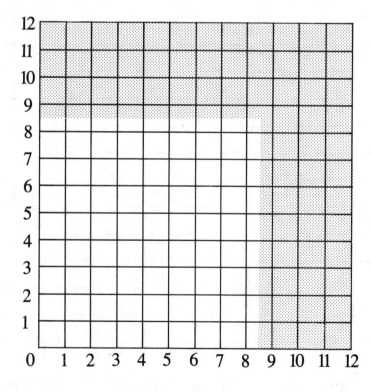

Using Coordinate Graphing

Mirror Image

Hold the edge of a mirror on the vertical lines in these letters.

A   M   H

1. Look in the mirror. Describe what you see.

_____

Each of these letters has a vertical line of **symmetry.**

2. Name some other capital letters with vertical lines

of symmetry. _____

3. Write a word in which every letter has a vertical line

of symmetry. _____

Hold the edge of a mirror on the horizontal lines in these letters.

B   E   C

4. Look in the mirror. Describe what you see. _____

_____

Each of these letters has a horizontal line of symmetry.

5. Name some other capital letters with horizonal lines

of symmetry. _____

6. Write a word in which every letter has a horizontal line

of symmetry. _____

Face Symmetry

Find a magazine with pictures.
Ask an adult to help you.

- Cut out a picture of a face.

- Cut the face in half vertically.

- Paste half of the face on this paper.

- Draw the other side of the face yourself.

Shape Cents

Here are the prices.

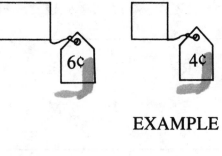

EXAMPLE

6¢ + 3¢ = 9¢

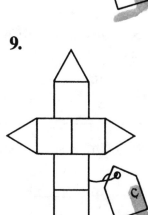

How much are these?

1.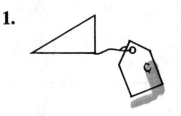

2.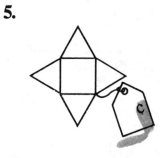

3.

4.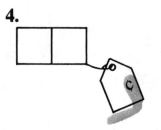

5.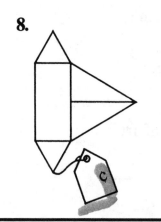

6.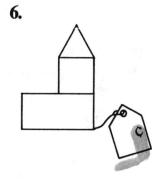

7.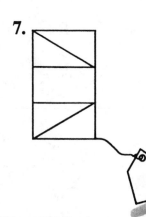

8.

9.

Hidden Shapes

This is a hidden quiz for you and your family.

Read the clue.

Use the letters as corners.

Connect the letters to make the shape,
and fill in the blank.

I am a rectangle and a drink.

I am ___MILK___.

```
M  .  K  .  R  .
I  .  L  .  Q  .
```

1. I am a triangle and a color.

I am _____ .

```
R  .  O  .  L  .
E  .  D  .  M  .
```

2. I am a triangle and an animal.

I am _____ .

```
S  .  M  .  A  .
P  .  C  .  T  .
```

3. I am a rectangle and a flower.

I am _____ .

```
M  .  S  .  R  .
A  .  O  .  E  .
```

4. I am a rectangle and a coin.

I am _____ .

```
D  .  N  .  I  .  P  .
M  .  L  .  E  .  Y  .
```

5. I am a square and a boy's name.

I am _____ .

```
J  .  N  .  R  .  D  .
O  .  H  .  A  .  T  .
```

6. I am a square and a piece of fruit.

I am _____ .

```
O  .  P  .  E  .  G  .
L  .  A  .  R  .
```

Riddle Stumpers

HOW ARE A KING AND A METER STICK ALIKE?

Write the letter of the square on the line above the fraction that tells what part of the square is shaded.

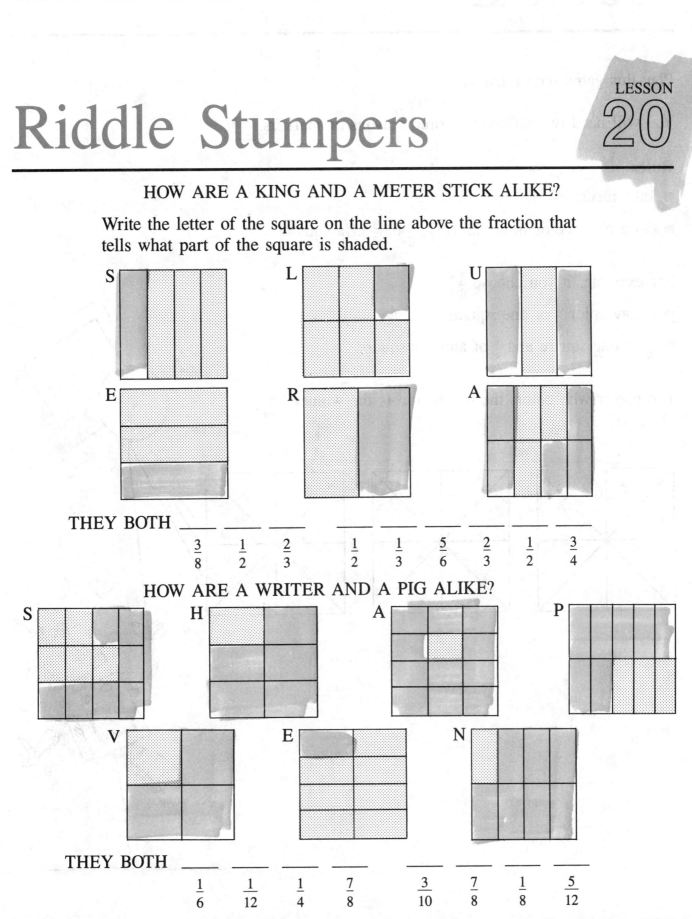

THEY BOTH ___ ___ ___   ___ ___ ___ ___ ___ ___

$\frac{3}{8}$ $\frac{1}{2}$ $\frac{2}{3}$ $\frac{1}{2}$ $\frac{1}{3}$ $\frac{5}{6}$ $\frac{2}{3}$ $\frac{1}{2}$ $\frac{3}{4}$

HOW ARE A WRITER AND A PIG ALIKE?

THEY BOTH ___ ___ ___ ___   ___ ___ ___ ___

$\frac{1}{6}$ $\frac{1}{12}$ $\frac{1}{4}$ $\frac{7}{8}$ $\frac{3}{10}$ $\frac{7}{8}$ $\frac{1}{8}$ $\frac{5}{12}$

Finding Fractional Parts of a Region

41

Color-In

Play this game with a friend.

You will need two different colored crayons or markers.

Rules

■ Take turns.

■ On a turn, color in a total of $\frac{1}{8}$, $\frac{2}{8}$ or $\frac{3}{8}$ of a square.

For example, if you choose $\frac{2}{8}$

you may color $\frac{2}{8}$ of one square

or $\frac{1}{8}$ of one square and $\frac{1}{8}$ of another square.

The player who colors the last region is the winner.

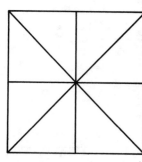 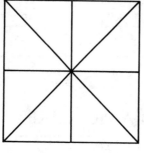

Finding Fractional Parts of a Region

Part of a Group

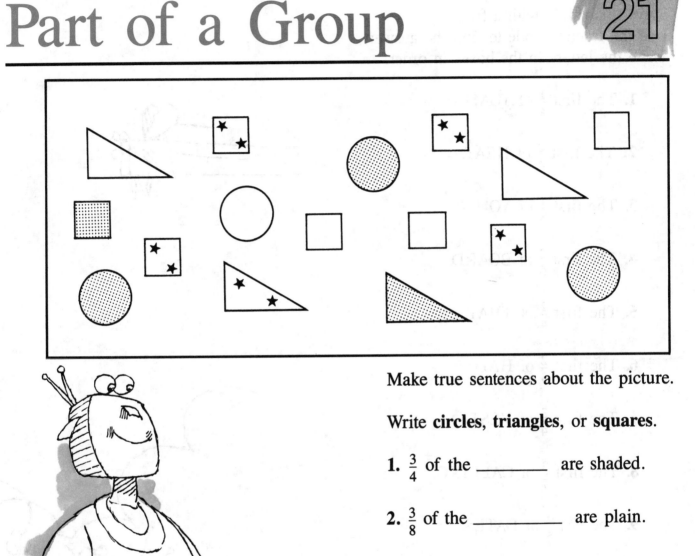

Make true sentences about the picture.

Write **circles**, **triangles**, or **squares**.

1. $\frac{3}{4}$ of the _____ are shaded.

2. $\frac{3}{8}$ of the _____ are plain.

3. $\frac{0}{4}$ of the _____ have stars.

4. $\frac{1}{4}$ of the _____ are shaded.

5. $\frac{2}{4}$ of the _____ are plain.

6. $\frac{4}{8}$ of the _____ have stars.

Fraction Code

HOW ARE A FISH AND A PIANO ALIKE?

Solve this riddle with a friend.
Use the fraction code to find the answer.
Write the letters in the boxes in order.

1. The first $\frac{1}{4}$ of TOAD.

2. The first $\frac{2}{4}$ of HEAT.

3. The first $\frac{1}{3}$ of YOU.

4. The first $\frac{2}{5}$ of BOARD.

5. The first $\frac{2}{4}$ of THAT.

6. The first $\frac{2}{3}$ of HAD.

7. The first $\frac{3}{4}$ of VEST.

8. The first $\frac{3}{7}$ of CALLING.

9. The last $\frac{2}{5}$ of DATES.

T												

Fraction Shapes

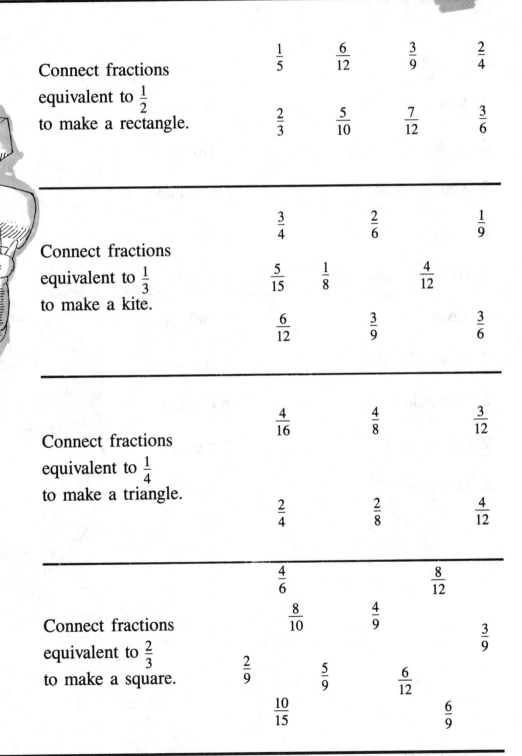

Connect fractions
equivalent to $\frac{1}{2}$
to make a rectangle.

$\frac{1}{5}$	$\frac{6}{12}$	$\frac{3}{9}$	$\frac{2}{4}$
$\frac{2}{3}$	$\frac{5}{10}$	$\frac{7}{12}$	$\frac{3}{6}$

Connect fractions
equivalent to $\frac{1}{3}$
to make a kite.

$\frac{3}{4}$ $\frac{2}{6}$ $\frac{1}{9}$

$\frac{5}{15}$ $\frac{1}{8}$ $\frac{4}{12}$

$\frac{6}{12}$ $\frac{3}{9}$ $\frac{3}{6}$

Connect fractions
equivalent to $\frac{1}{4}$
to make a triangle.

$\frac{4}{16}$ $\frac{4}{8}$ $\frac{3}{12}$

$\frac{2}{4}$ $\frac{2}{8}$ $\frac{4}{12}$

Connect fractions
equivalent to $\frac{2}{3}$
to make a square.

$\frac{4}{6}$ $\frac{8}{12}$

$\frac{8}{10}$ $\frac{4}{9}$

$\frac{3}{9}$

$\frac{2}{9}$ $\frac{5}{9}$ $\frac{6}{12}$

$\frac{10}{15}$ $\frac{6}{9}$

A Capital Quiz

This is a quiz for you and your family.
How many state capitals do you know?
  Guess first.
  Then draw lines and match equivalent fractions
  to check your guesses.

State	Capital
1. Montana $\frac{2}{3}$	$\frac{3}{15}$ Boston
2. Georgia $\frac{1}{2}$	$\frac{10}{12}$ Dover
3. Massachusetts $\frac{1}{5}$	$\frac{3}{9}$ Columbia
4. Ohio $\frac{3}{4}$	$\frac{2}{16}$ Denver
5. Alaska $\frac{2}{5}$	$\frac{2}{12}$ Austin
6. Texas $\frac{1}{6}$	$\frac{4}{6}$ Helena
7. South Carolina $\frac{1}{3}$	$\frac{4}{10}$ Juneau
8. Colorado $\frac{1}{8}$	$\frac{9}{12}$ Columbus
9. California $\frac{1}{4}$	$\frac{6}{12}$ Atlanta
10. Delaware $\frac{5}{6}$	$\frac{2}{8}$ Sacramento

Finding Equivalent Fractions

Mystery Number

Write the number for each word name.
Cross off the number in the cloud.
The number that is left is the mystery number.

25.1	47.82	14.02	9.36	6.9
20.01	5.7	60.43	70.05	5.07	20.10
15.04	8.7	10.1	8.17	14.2

1. five and seven tenths _____

2. six and nine tenths _____

3. fourteen and two tenths _____

4. twenty-five and one tenth _____

5. eight and seventeen hundredths _____

6. nine and thirty-six hundredths _____

7. fifteen and four hundredths _____

8. forty-seven and eighty-two hundredths _____

9. eight and seven tenths _____

10. sixty and forty-three hundredths _____

11. seventy and five hundredths _____

12. fourteen and two hundredths _____

13. five and seven hundredths _____

14. ten and one tenth _____

15. twenty and ten hundredths _____

THE MYSTERY NUMBER IS _____

Sports Facts

This is a sports trivia quiz for you and your family.
First try to answer the questions.
Then check by matching the word name with the number.
The number gives the answer to the question. Ring the
correct answer.

1. Four and six tenths

How many rings are on the Olympic flag?
4.6   There is 1 ring.
4.06   There are 3 rings.
4.6   There are 5 rings.
0.46   There are 7 rings.

2. Three and eleven hundredths

How many pins are in the back row of bowling?
3.11   There are 4 pins.
31.1   There are 5 pins.
311   There are 8 pins.
0.311   There are 10 pins.

3. Six and eight hundredths

What is the distance between bases on a baseball diamond?
6.8   The distance is 100 feet.
6.08   The distance is 90 feet.
0.68   The distance is 60 feet.
68   The distance is 50 feet.

4. Twelve and one tenth

How many yards long is a football field from goal post to
goal post?
1.21   The field is 100 yards long.
121   The field is 300 yards long.
12.1   The field is 120 yards long.
0.121   The field is 150 yards long.

5. Forty and two hundredths

Who holds the lifetime record for batting the most
homeruns?
402   Lou Gehrig
4.02   Willie Mays
40.2   Babe Ruth
40.02   Hank Aaron

Decimal Locksmith

The number on the lock is the target number.
Put an **X** on the two keys with numbers whose sum or difference
is the target number.

1.

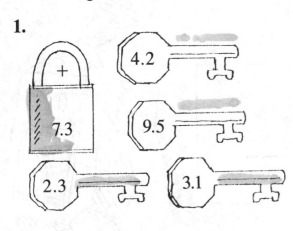

2.

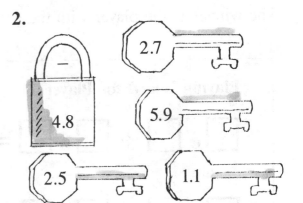

3.

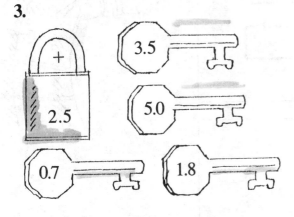

4.

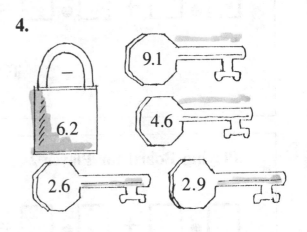

5.

6.

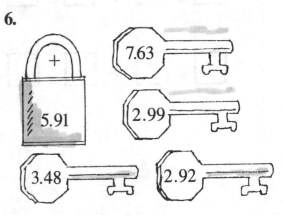

Adding and Subtracting Decimals

Decimal Play-offs

Ask someone to play this game with you.
You need 1 number cube and 2 pencils.

- Take turns.

- Roll the number cube.
  Write the number in one of the squares on your playing board.

- After the squares are filled in, add across.
  Then add to find the total.

The winner is the player with the greater total.

Playing Board for Player 1

$$\square . \square + \square . \square = \underline{\hspace{3cm}}$$

$$\square . \square + \square . \square = \underline{\hspace{3cm}}$$

TOTAL ☐

Playing Board for Player 2

$$\square . \square + \square . \square = \underline{\hspace{3cm}}$$

$$\square . \square + \square . \square = \underline{\hspace{3cm}}$$

TOTAL ☐

Adding and Subtracting Decimals

Collections of Money

Six children emptied their pockets.
The pictures show the coins they have.
Tell how much money each child has.

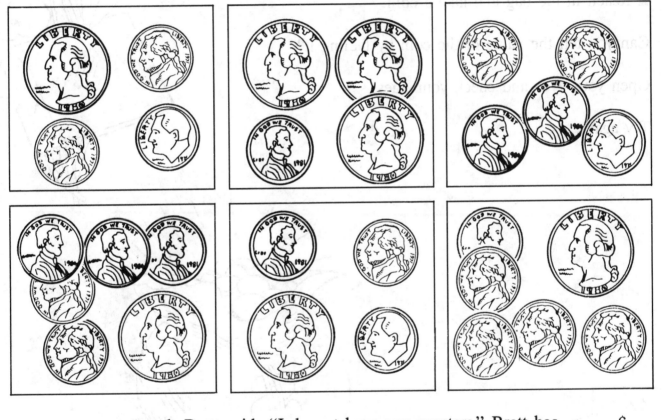

1. Brett said, "I do not have any quarters." Brett has _____ ¢.

2. Juan said, "All of my coins are different." Juan has _____ ¢.

3. Maria said, "I have more than one quarter." Maria has _____ ¢.

4. Carla said, "I do not have any pennies." Carla has _____ ¢.

5. Jason said, "I have four nickels." Jason has _____ ¢.

6. Lisa said, "I have more pennies than nickels." Lisa has _____ ¢.

Money Bags

Ask an adult to help you with this activity.
You need a paper bag and some coins.
Try to use at least 1 quarter, 1 dime, 1 nickel, and 1 penny.

- Put the coins in the paper bag.

- Close your eyes.

- Shake the bag.

- Reach in the bag and take a coin.

Can you tell the value of the coin by feeling it?

Open your eyes and check your guess.

Try again.

Using Money

Baseball Stars

The table shows the number of home runs made by some baseball players in their careers.

Home Run Leaders

Player	Number of Home Runs
Hank Aaron	755
Reggie Jackson	548
Harmon Killebrew	573
Mickey Mantle	536
Willie Mays	660
Frank Robinson	586
Babe Ruth	714

Use the information in the table to answer these questions.

1. How many home runs did Babe Ruth score?

_____

2. How many home runs did Reggie Jackson score?

_____

3. Who scored more home runs, Frank Robinson or Mickey Mantle?

_____

4. Who scored the greatest number of home runs?

_____

5. How many more home runs did Willie Mays score than Harmon Killebrew?

_____

6. How many more home runs did Babe Ruth score than Reggie Jackson?

_____

What Color Cars Go By?

Ask an adult to help you.

Watch 25 cars go by. Make a tally mark for the color of each car.

Color	
Black	
Blue	
Green	
Grey	
Red	
White	
Yellow	

Use the tally marks to make a table.

■ Write the name of each color.

■ Write the total number of cars for each color.

1. The greatest number of cars are the color _____ .

2. The least number of cars are the color _____ .

Color of Cars

Color	Number of Cars

Making a Table

Sam's Super Sandwiches

The bar graph shows what sandwiches Sam sold in one month.

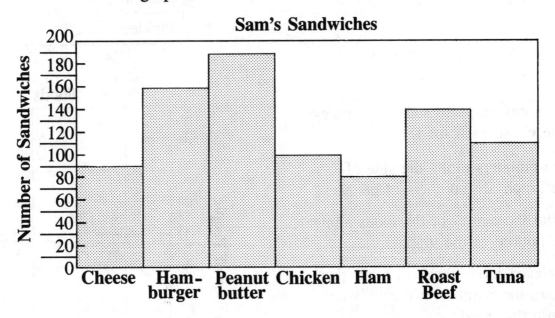

Sam's Sandwiches

Use the information in the bar graph to fill in the numbers in these sentences.

1. Sam sold _____ roast beef sandwiches.
He sold _____ cheese sandwiches.
He sold _____ chicken sandwiches.

2. Sam sold _____ hamburger sandwiches.
He sold _____ more hamburger sandwiches than chicken sandwiches.

3. Sam sold _____ tuna sandwiches.
He sold _____ more tuna sandwiches than ham sandwiches.

4. Sam sold _____ peanut butter sandwiches.
He sold _____ more peanut butter sandwiches than cheese sandwiches.

Peanut Butter And ?

Conduct a **survey**.

- Ask 20 people to tell which of these foods they like best with peanut butter.

- Make a tally for each choice.

Foods

Jelly
Apple
Banana
Marshmallow
Pickles

Make a bar graph to show how many people chose each food.

- The numbers along the side of the graph are numbers of people.

- Write the names of the foods along the bottom of the graph.

- For each food, shade in a bar that shows the number of people who chose that food.

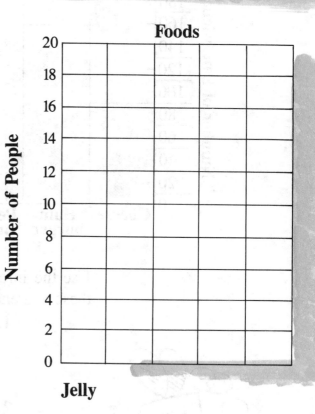

Foods

Number of People

20
18
16
14
12
10
8
6
4
2
0

Jelly

The greatest number of people like peanut butter and _____ .

Secret Codes

Use the clues to find each person's secret code.

2,136	9,822	6,847
4,346	3,346	2,946

1. Mia

My code has
a 7 in the ones
place. My code is

_____.

2. Kim

The sum of the
digits in my code
is 16. My code is

_____.

3. Bob

My code has an 8
in the hundreds
place. My code is

_____.

4. Ronald

My code has a 2
in the thousands
place. My code is

_____.

5. Tanya

My code is
less than Ronald's
code. My code is

_____.

6. Tony

My code is
greater than Kim's
code. My code is

_____.

The Between Game

Play this game with a friend.

One player is the **thinker**.
The thinker thinks of a mystery number between 1 and 500.

The other player is the **guesser**.
The guesser tries to guess the mystery number by asking "between" questions.

Is the number between 250 and 500?

No. Guess again.

When the guesser knows the mystery number,
the guesser says, **"The mystery number is . . ."**

Keep track of the number of questions.

1. What was the mystery number? _____

2. How many questions did you ask? _____

Using Logical Reasoning

Make Sense

Use the numbers on the signs to finish these stories.
Be sure that the numbers you choose make sense in the stories.

1. Sandy likes to play checkers with her mother.
They played _____ games. Sandy won
more games than her mother. Sandy won
_____ games. Her mother won _____ games.

2. Tom went bowling. He scored _____ points
in the first game. He scored 20 more points in
the second game than in the first game. Tom
scored _____ points in the second game.
Tom scored a total of _____ points in the
two games.

3. Jane played a ring toss game. She scored the
most points in the first game. She scored _____
points in the first game. She scored 10 points less
in the second game. Jane scored _____ points
in the second game. She scored _____ points
in the third game.

4. Sandy, Tom and Jane played beanbag toss. Sandy
scored _____ points. Tom scored twice as many
points as Sandy. Tom scored _____ points.
Jane scored 2 points less than Tom. Jane scored
_____ points.

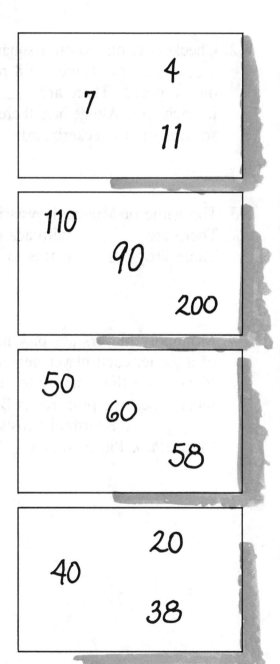

Game Facts

Find some people who like to play games.
Work together to fill in the numbers.
The numbers must fit the facts about the game.

1. The game of checkers is a game for _____ players.
   At the beginning of the game, each player has
   _____ checkers. Altogether, there are _____
   checkers.

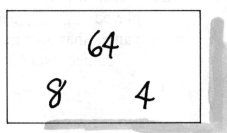

2. Checkers is played on a square board that has
   _____ sides. There are 8 rows of small squares
   on the board. There are _____ small squares
   in each row. Altogether, there are _____ small
   squares on a checkerboard.

64
8   4

3. The game of Monopoly was invented in _____ .
   There are _____ railroads on the Monopoly board.
   There are _____ places to land on the board.

40
1933
4

4. Monopoly players use play money. At the beginning
   of a game, each player gets a total of $ _____ .
   Players use their money to buy property. The
   most expensive property is Boardwalk. It costs
   $ _____ . Boardwalk costs $50 more than Park
   Place. Park Place costs $ _____ .

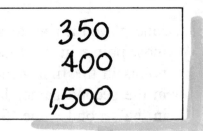

350
400
1,500

Shopping Questions

Write a question for each story.
Then use the facts in the story to answer the question.

Mrs. Green bought 3 pairs of sunglasses
for $5 each. She bought an umbrella for $9.

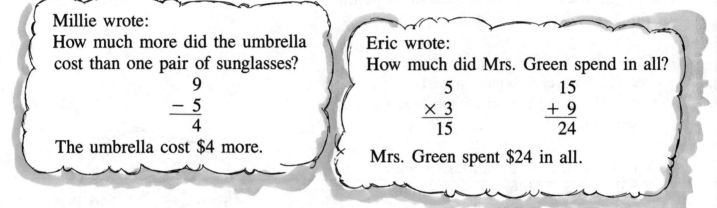

Millie wrote:
How much more did the umbrella
cost than one pair of sunglasses?

$$\begin{array}{r} 9 \\ -\ 5 \\ \hline 4 \end{array}$$

The umbrella cost $4 more.

Eric wrote:
How much did Mrs. Green spend in all?

$$\begin{array}{r} 5 \\ \times\ 3 \\ \hline 15 \end{array} \qquad \begin{array}{r} 15 \\ +\ 9 \\ \hline 24 \end{array}$$

Mrs. Green spent $24 in all.

1. Bob bought 3 pounds of bananas for $.99. He also bought a cantelope for $.79.

2. Ann had $8.00. She bought a hat for $4.00. She bought a scarf for $2.75.

3. Dr. Hart bought a sweater for $29, a shirt for $21, and a tie for $18.

4. Mrs. Grady gave $8 to Sue and $8 to Jeff. Sue bought stickers for $2.00.

5. Todd bought 2 boxes of muffins for $1.20 each. One box had 12 bran muffins. The other box had 6 blueberry muffins.

6. Sandy bought 2 dozen flowers. Ten of the flowers were mums. Eight of the flowers were carnations. The rest of the flowers were roses.

Oodles Of Questions

2 or 3 people can play this game.

Set a time limit of 3 minutes for each story.

Each player should:
- Write lots of questions for each story.
- Answer the questions.
- Check the answers with the other players.
- Score 1 point for each question with a right answer.

The player with the greatest number of points for the four stories is the winner.

1. There are 26 bones in each of your feet. There are 27 bones in each hand. There are a total of 206 bones in your body.

2. A raw carrot has 21 calories. A stalk of celery has 5 calories. A medium green pepper has three times as many calories as a stalk of celery.

3. A dollar bill is about 16 centimeters long. It is about 7 centimeters wide. A dollar bill costs about 1¢ to produce.

4. A crab has 10 legs. A spider has 8 legs. An ant has 4 less legs than a crab.

Writing Questions

Make It Even

Draw a line through each sign.
The total amount of money on each
side of the line must be the same.

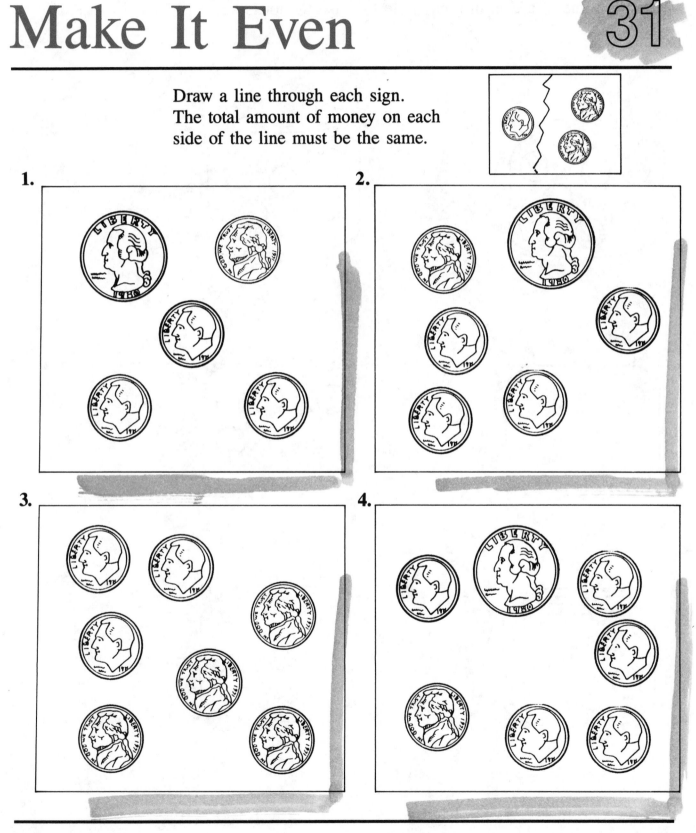

1.

2.

3.

4.

Money In The Jar

Work with a friend.

Write the value of a coin in each circle to make the totals correct.

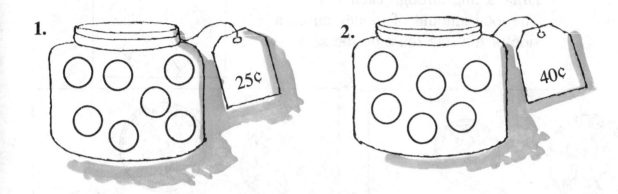

1.  25¢

2. 40¢

3. 75¢

4.  50¢

5. 60¢

6. 45¢

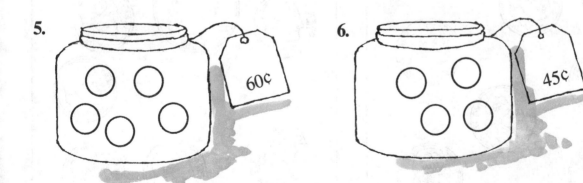

Guessing and Checking

Enrichment
MATH

Grade 3
Answer Key and Teaching Suggestions

AMERICAN EDUCATION PUBLISHING

OVERVIEW

ENRICHMENT MATH was developed to provide children with additional opportunities to practice and review mathematical concepts and skills and to use these skills in the home. Children work individually on the first page of each lesson and then with family members on the second page. Every lesson presents high interest activities designed to heighten children's awareness of mathematical ideas and to enrich their understanding of those ideas.

ENRICHMENT MATH consists of 31 two page lessons at grade levels 1 through 6. At each grade level *ENRICHMENT MATH* covers all of the important topics of the traditional mathematics curriculum. Each lesson is filled with games, puzzles and other opportunities for exploring mathematical ideas.

AUTHORS

Peggy Kaye is the author of *Games For Math* and *Games for Reading.* She spent ten years as a classroom teacher in New York City public and private schools, and is today a private tutor in math and reading.

Carole Greenes is Professor of Mathematics at Boston University. She has taught mathematics and mathematics education for more than 20 years and is a former elementary school teacher. Dr. Greenes is the author of a K-8 basal math series and has also written for programs such as *Reach Program, Trivia Math* and the *TOPS-Problem.*

Linda Schulman is Professor of Mathematics at Lesley College . For the past 12 years, she has taught courses in mathematics and mathematics education. Prior to her work at the college level, Dr. Schulman taught elementary school. She is the author of a basal mathematics textbook as well as of other curriculum programs including *TOPS-Problem Solving Program, The Mathworks* and *How to Solve Story Problems.*

WHY ENRICHMENT MATH?

Enrichment and parental involvement are both crucial parts of children's education. More school systems are recognizing that this part of the educational process is crucial to school success. Enrichment activities give children the opportunity to practice basic skills and that encourages them to think mathematically. That's exactly the kind of opportunity children get when doing *ENRICHMENT MATH.*

One of the important goals of *ENRICHMENT MATH* is to increase children's involvement in mathematics and mathematical concepts. When children are involved in mathematics activities, they become more alert and receptive to learning. They understand more. They remember more. Games, puzzles, and "hands-on" activities that lead to mathematical discoveries are guaranteed to get children involved in mathematics. That's why such activities form the core of each *ENRICHMENT MATH* lesson.

Another important goal of *ENRICHMENT MATH* is to provide opportunities for parents to become involved in their children's education. Every *ENRICHMENT MATH* lesson has two parts. First, there is a lesson that the children do on their own. Second, there is a game or an activity that the child does with an adult. *ENRICHMENT MATH* doesn't ask parents to teach children. Instead the program asks parents to play math games and engage in interesting math activities with their children.

Published in 1995 by AMERICAN EDUCATION PUBLISHING
© 1991 SRA/McGraw-Hill

HOW TO USE ENRICHMENT MATH

Each *ENRICHMENT MATH* book consists of 31 lessons on perforated sheets. On the front of each sheet, there is an activity that the child completes independently. On the back there is a follow-up activity for the child to complete with an adult. These group activities include games, projects, puzzles, surveys and trivia quizzes. The front and back pages of a lesson focus on the same mathematical skill.

Activities may be done at the time the skills are being taught to provide additional practice, or used at a later date to maintain skill levels.

Within each book, the lessons are organized into four or five sections. These sections correspond to the major mathematical topics emphasized at the particular grade level. This means you can quickly locate a lesson on whatever topic you want at whatever level is appropriate for your child. Let's say your first-grader is working on addition in school. You can feel confident that the first several lessons in the addition and subtraction section will have something suited to your needs.

Also Available—ENRICHMENT READING

Overview

ENRICHMENT READING is designed to provide children with practice in reading and to increase their reading abilities. The program consists of six books, one each for grade levels 1 through 6. The major areas of reading instruction—word skills, vocabulary, study skills, and literary forms—are covered as appropriate at each level.

ENRICHMENT READING provides a wide range of activities that target a variety of skills in each instructional area. The program is unique because it helps children expand their skills in playful ways with games, puzzles, riddles, contests, and stories. The high-interest activities are informative and fun to do.

Home and parental involvement is important to any child's success in school. *ENRICHMENT READING* is the ideal vehicle for fostering home involvement. Every lesson provides specific opportunities for children to work with a parent, a family member, an adult, or a friend.

LOOK FOR *ENRICHMENT READING* and *ENRICHMENT MATH* at stores that carry Master Skills.

Also Available from American Education Publishing—

BRIGHTER CHILD™ SOFTWARE

The Brighter Child™ Software series is a set of innovative programs designed to teach basic reading, phonics, and math skills in a fun and engaging way to children ages 3 - 9.

Muppet™/Brighter Child™ Software available on CD-ROM
*Same & Different	Sorting & Ordering
*Letters: Capital & Small	Thinking Skills
*Beginning Sounds: Phonics	Sound Patterns: More Phonics

also available on diskette

Brighter Child™ Software available on CD-ROM and diskette
Math Grade 1	Math Grade 2	Math Grade 3
Reading Grade 1	Reading Grade 2	Reading Grade 3

•call (800) 542-7833 for more information

Brighter Child™ Software Available at Stores Near You

TEACHING SUGGESTIONS
Grade 3
Optional Activities

A TIP FOR SUCCESS

Children will find *ENRICHMENT MATH* Grade 3 assignments enjoyable and easy to understand. Although each lesson has simple and easy-to-read instructions, you may wish to spend a few minutes explaining some lessons before assigning the material. You might even do some of the activities prior to giving the assignments. Many of the activities can liven up an at-home math session and will prepare your child for even greater success.

Part One: Computation–Basic Facts

ENRICHMENT MATH Grade 3 has five lessons on the basic facts. Traditionally, grade 3 is the level at which students should master the basic addition and subtraction facts and begin to address the challenge of mastering the basic multiplication and division facts.

The first two lessons in this section deal with basic addition and subtraction facts and are appropriate for use at the beginning of the school year. You may wish to introduce the first lesson, *Target Sum*, by writing a sum, any number from 0 to 18, and asking your child to give all the pairs of addends with this sum. The games provided in these lessons, or some variations of them, can be used throughout the year to help your child master and retain the basic addition and subtraction facts.

The second pair of lessons in this section deal with basic multiplication and division facts and are appropriate for use whenever your child is studying these facts. The lesson *Nines-By-Fingers* presents a mechanical way to find products when multiplying by 9. As a follow-up to this lesson, you may want your child to look for a pattern in the digits that name the product of 9 and another whole number: The sum of the digits is always nine. This discovery will help students master their multiplication facts with 9 as a factor.

The game *Roll-A-Product* can be used often throughout the year as an enjoyable way to practice the basic multiplication facts. A variation of the game that includes all of the basic facts can be created as follows. Use 20 small squares of paper to make 2 sets of playing pieces on which you have written the digits from 0 to 9. The playing pieces are placed face down and players take turns selecting two and multiplying the numbers drawn. The product should be written on a playing board if the appropriate space is empty. Different playing boards can be made by drawing a 5 x 5 array of boxes and filling in the top row and left column with any 4 digits chosen at random. Your child should use a different card for each new game so that he or she eventually practices all of the facts.

Part Two: Place Value and Operations with Whole Numbers

This section of *ENRICHMENT MATH* Grade 3 extends computational work with whole numbers from basic facts to adding and subtracting up to 4-digit numbers and multiplying and dividing 2-digit numbers by 1-digit numbers. Through a series of interesting puzzles, games, and quizzes, your child is provided with numerous opportunities to improve his or her skills with basic operations. Some of the games, such as *199* and *Divvy Up*, can be used thoughout the year as an interesting way to practice and maintain computational skills.

This part of the program also gives attention to the concept of place value, important for children to understand because of its importance to the procedures, or algorithms, utilized when computing with numbers larger than a single digit. You might choose to allow your child to play the game *Place It Right* throughout the year as free time permits. Variations of the game can be devised, if you wish. For example, your child can pick four cards and with them name the greatest and the least numbers possible. Another variation, after adding or subtracting of 2-digit numbers has been introduced and practiced, is to use the four cards to name two 2-digit addends that have the greatest sum or the least sum.

Part Three: Measurement and Geometry

Six lessons are included in this section that deal with measurement concepts such as time, metric units, and customary units and geometric concepts such as coordinate graphing, symmetry, and the identification of shapes. These lessons can be used any time.

The first three lessons are designed to help your child develop a sense of the concepts and skills involved in measurement. One of the important objectives is to help children to develop a mental model of a unit of measure. For example, in the lesson *Measure Up*, children use a piece of string one meter, or less than one meter in length. Once found, a mental picture of these objects can be kept in mind and used when needed in the future to compare with and estimate the length of other objects.

Part Four: Fractions and Decimals

The first two lessons in this section deal with fractional parts of an object and fractional parts of a set. An extension of these lessons would be to have your child separate a circle or square or other geometric figure into fractional parts and to color the parts to create an interesting design.

The lesson on *Fraction Shapes* and *A Capital Quiz* provides interesting practice with equivalent fractions, an important concept for children to understand in order to add and subtract unlike fractions at a later point in their studies.

The next two lessons present activities with decimals, including adding and subtracting decimals. The final lesson on amounts of money is included at this point since our monetary system is primarily a decimal system, and a better understanding of one system reinforces understanding of the other.

Part Five: Problem Solving

The final six lessons in *ENRICHMENT MATH* Grade 3 address problem solving. The first two lessons deal with information found in tables or graphs. This is particularly important for a child to understand since much of the information that is made available to citizens today is done through graphical devices such as tables and bar graphs. The lesson *What Color Cars Go By* introduces children to one way that data are collected and recorded.

To complete the activities in the remaining lessons, children will apply logical reasoning, use their number sense, write their own problems, and apply the problem-solving strategy of guess and check. It is important that the strategy guess-and-check be introduced at an early level so that children can begin to see the difference between "wild" guesses and "intelligent" guesses and to learn how to look for patterns in the results of their guesses in order to make their next guess a more appropriate one.

Answer Key
Grade 3–ENRICHMENT MATH

page 3:

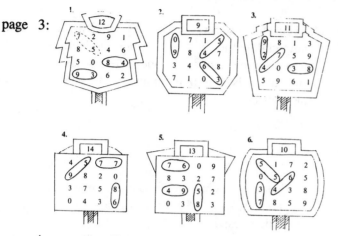

page 4: answers will vary.

page 5: 1. 8 2. 6 3. 4 4. 18 5. 13 6. 9
7. 16 8. 0 9. 11 10. 7 11. 12
12. 8, 5

page 6: answers will vary.

page 7: 1. 45 2. 6 3. 72 4. 81 5. 27 6. 54

page 8:

Playing Board

×	1	2	3	4	5	6
1	1	2	3	4	5	6
2	2	4	6	8	10	12
3	3	6	9	12	15	18
4	4	8	12	16	20	24
5	5	10	15	20	25	30
6	6	12	18	24	30	36

page 9:

1.

24	÷	6	=	4
÷		÷		÷
8	÷	2	=	4
=		=		=
3	÷	3	=	1

2.

36	÷	6	=	6
÷		÷		÷
9	÷	3	=	3
=		=		=
6	÷	2	=	3

3.

48	÷	6	=	8
÷		÷		÷
8	÷	2	=	4
=		=		=
6	÷	3	=	2

4.

40	÷	4	=	10
÷		÷		÷
8	÷	4	=	2
=		=		=
5	÷	1	=	5

page 10: 1. answers will vary 2. 4
3. answers will vary 4. 5
5. answers will vary 6. 5

page 11: 1. $7 \times 4 = 28$; $9 \times 6 = 54$
2. $9 + 7 = 16$; $18 \div 6 = 3$
3. $12 - 5 = 7$; $13 - 9 = 4$
4. $24 \div 8 = 3$; $7 + 4 = 11$
5. $8 \times 0 = 0$; $36 \div 6 = 6$

page 12: answers will vary

page 13:

1.

5	+	7	=	12
×		+		−
3	×	2	=	6
=		=		=
15	−	9	=	6

2.

18	÷	6	=	3
÷		−		+
2	×	4	=	8
=		=		=
9	+	2	=	11

3.

7	×	2	=	14
+		×		+
6	÷	3	=	2
=		=		=
13	−	6	=	7

4.

24	÷	3	=	8
÷		−		−
6	÷	2	=	3
=		=		=
4	+	1	=	5

page 14: answers will vary

page 15: 1. 3782 2. 4590 3. 9852 4. 1627
5. 6534 6. 9107

page 16: with any set of 4 number cards you can make 24 different numbers.

page 17: 1. bus 2. toy car, van 3. truck, dune buggy 4. taxi, van 5. truck, bus, dune buggy 6. vans

page 18: answers will vary

page 19: answers will vary

page 20: 1. 112; whale shark 2. 143; ostrich
3. 616; St. Bernard 4. 1853; goby
5. 1200; Helena's hummingbird
6. 7000; yorkshire terrier

page 21:

¹1	9	²1		³4	5
3	⁴7	9	6		
2		8	⁵5	5	
⁶4	⁷9			6	
	⁸8	⁹7	¹⁰2		¹¹6
¹²6	0	5	3		2
	1		¹³4	2	9

page 22: answers will vary

page 23: 1. 3 2. 4 3. 8 4. 5 5. 7 6. 9

page 24: 1. $34 \times 2 = 68$ 2. $15 \times 3 = 45$
3. $14 \times 5 = 70$ 4. $26 \times 3 = 78$

page 25: 1. 44 2. 30 3. 50 4. 32 5. 36
6. 42 7. 32 8. 18 9. kangaroo
10. pig, opposum, hedge hog, dog

page 26: answers will vary

page 27:

START	ARROWS	STOP
2	↑	12
14	↑	24
38	↑	48
15	→	16
31	→	32
42	←	41
57	←	56
25	↓	15
39	↓ →	30
6	↑↑	26
21	↓ → →	13
80	↓↓↓←	49
38	↑↑↑→	69

START	ARROWS	STOP
3	↑	13
35	↑↑	55
64	↓↓	44
32	→ →	35
76	→ → →	73
7	↑↑→	26
52	↓↓↓↓ → →	14
19	↑↑↑↑↑↑→ →	85
22	↑ → →	34
98	↓↓↓↓ → →	56
62	↑↑↑ → → →	95
16	↑↑↑↑↑	66
37	↑↑↑↑↑ → → →	80

page 28: answers will vary

page 29: 1. 8 2. 30 3. 22 4. 6 5. 26 6. 21

page 30: answers will vary

page 31: answers will vary

page 32: 1. 300 2. 91 3. 160 4. 270 5. 340
6. 400 7. 61 8. 46

page 33: 1. years 2. pounds 3. feet 4. days
5. quart 6. miles 7. minutes 8. hours

page 34: answers will vary

page 35:

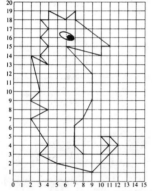

page 36: answers will vary

page 37: 1. answers will vary
2. I, O, T, U, V, W, X, Y
3. answers will vary 4. answers will
vary 5. D, H, I, O, X 6. answers
will vary

page 38: answers will vary

page 39: 1. 3¢ 2. 1¢ 3. 5¢ 4. 8¢ 5. 8¢
6. 11¢ 7. 18¢ 8. 14¢ 9. 23¢

page 40: 1. RED 2. CAT 3. ROSE 4. DIME
5. JOHN 6. PEAR

page 41: THEY BOTH ARE RULERS; THEY BOTH
HAVE PENS.

page 42: answers will vary

page 43: 1. circles 2. squares 3. circles
4. triangles 5. triangles 6. squares

page 44: 2. HEat 3. You 4. BOard 5. THat
6. HAd 7. VESt 8. CALling
9. datES;... THEY BOTH HAVE SCALES.

page 45:

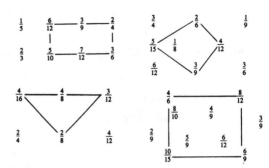

page 46: 1. $\frac{4}{6}$ Helena 2. $\frac{6}{12}$ Atlanta
3. $\frac{3}{15}$ Boston 4. $\frac{9}{12}$ Columbus
5. $\frac{4}{10}$ Juneau 6. $\frac{2}{12}$ Austin
7. $\frac{3}{9}$ Columbia 8. $\frac{2}{16}$ Denver
9. $\frac{2}{8}$ Sacramento 10. $\frac{10}{12}$ Dover

page 47: 1. 5.7 2. 6.9 3. 14.2 4. 25.1
5. 8.17 6. 9.36 7. 15.04 8. 47.82
9. 8.7 10. 60.43 11. 70.05
12. 14.02 13. 5.07 14. 10.1
15. 20.10; Mystery number is 20.01.

page 48: 1. There are 5 rings. 2. There are 4
pins. 3. The distance is 90 feet.
4. The field is 120 yards long. 5. Hank
Aaron

page 49: 1. 4.2; 3.1 2. 5.9; 1.1 3. 0.7; 1.8
4. 9.1; 2.9 5. 5.08; 1.24
6. 2.99; 2.92

page 50: answers will vary

page 51: 1. 22¢ 2. 41¢ 3. 76¢ 4. 45¢
5. 46¢ 6. 38¢

page 52: answers will vary

page 53: 1. 714 2. 548 3. Frank Robinson
4. Hank Aaron 5. 87 6. 166

page 54: answers will vary

page 55: 1. 140; 90; 100 2. 160; 60 3. 110; 30
4. 190; 70

page 56: answers will vary

page 57: 1. 6847 2. 3346 3. 9822 4. 2946
5. 2136 6. 4346

page 58: answers will vary

page 59: 1. 11; 7; 4   2. 90; 110; 200   3. 60; 50; 58   4. 20; 40; 38

page 60: 1. 2; 12; 24   2. 4; 8; 64   3. 1933; 4; 40   4. 1500; 400; 350

page 61: answers will vary

page 62: answers will vary

page 63:

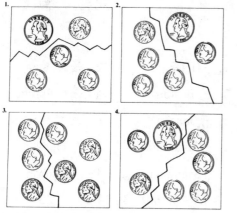

page 64:

Also available from American Education Publishing—

MASTER SKILLS SERIES SKILL BOOKS

The Master Skills Series is not just another workbook series. These full-color workbooks were designed by experts who understand the value of reinforcing basic skills! Subjects include Reading, Math, English, Comprehension, Spelling and Writing, and Thinking Skills.

• 88 pages   • 40 titles   • All-color   • $5.95 each